DIY
FEARLESS FASHION

MAKEUP MAGIC
WITH GLAM AND GORE BEAUTY

By Rebecca Rissman

COMPASS POINT BOOKS
a capstone imprint

Compass Point Books are published by Capstone
1710 Roe Crest Drive, North Mankato, Minnesota 56003
www.capstonepub.com

Library of Congress Cataloging-in-Publication Data
Library of Congress Cataloging-in-Publication data is available on the
Library of Congress website.
ISBN 978-1-5435-1098-0 (library binding)
ISBN 978-0-7565-6096-6 (eBook PDF)

Editorial Credits
Mandy Robbins, editor; Heather Kindseth and Heidi Thompson, designers;
Tracy Cummins, media researcher; Marcy Morin and Sarah Schuette,
photo stylists; Jazlin Honeycutt, makeup artist; Kathy McColley,
production specialist

Photo Credits
Images by Capstone Studio: Karon Dubke, except:
Shutterstock: Chursina Viktoriia, 24, FlyIntoSpace, 12, Galina F, 13, Jane
Kelly, 9, Kozak Dmytro, 19, Kseniia Perminova, 7, okawa somchai, 4–5,
Sunspire, Design Element

Printed and bound in the USA
PA017

TABLE OF CONTENTS

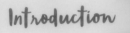

BE ADVENTUROUS!

Glitter eye shadow? Check.

Plum lipstick? Check.

False lashes? Check.

Fierce attitude? Check!

Your makeup kit isn't just a cosmetics collection. It's your ticket to adventure. Use the looks in this book to push your own creativity. Mix and match them. Try out different colors. Add something that is bold and uniquely you. Grab a few friends and create these bold looks together.

BEFORE YOU START CREATING, GATHER SOME SUPPLIES:

variety of eye shadows
eyelash glue
false eyelashes
foundation
gentle facial cleanser
lipstick in bright, fun colors
makeup brushes, sponges, or applicators
mascara
pencil and liquid eyeliner

PATCH TEST

Before you start slathering a new product on your face, do a patch test. Spread a small amount on your inner elbow or behind your ear. Then wait a full 24 hours. If any signs of redness or irritation show up, don't use the product. You probably have a sensitivity or allergy to something in it.

A CLEAN CANVAS

Wash your face with a gentle cleanser before trying any of the looks in this book. Doing this will ensure any residual makeup is cleaned off. It will also keep your skin healthy. If your skin feels dry after you wash it, apply a facial moisturizer before using any makeup.

CONTOURING MAGIC

For many makeup artists, the first step in any look is preparing their "canvas." In this case, the canvas is your face. Preparation may include contouring. Contouring can highlight your best features. You don't have to be a professional makeup artist to do it. Try this bold base look at your next formal event for a wow-worthy look.

STEPS:

1. Use your fingers to apply a thin base of your regular foundation all over your face.

2. With the beauty blender, apply darker foundation at your temples, along both cheekbones, below your jaw, and just under the center of your lower lip. If you have a big forehead, you might add more dark color along your hairline.

3. Dip your beauty blender in warm water and wring it out so that it is slightly damp. Tap the large end of the beauty blender gently against your skin to blend your contour color in well. Don't rub back and forth.

4. Rinse out the beauty blender. Then use it to apply your lighter color below your eyes, down the outer edges of your nose, and up on a diagonal just past your outer eyes. This will form a large triangle of light color beneath each eye.

5. Add more of the light color along the bridge of your nose and at the center of your chin.

6. Use the beauty blender to blend the light color in well.

7. Apply blush to the apples of your cheeks using the large makeup brush.

8. Wipe the blush off the large makeup brush on a tissue, and use it to apply transparent powder all over your face to set the look.

THE SECRET TO THE SMOKY EYE

WHAT YOU NEED:

eye shadow primer

small and medium sized eye shadow brushes

shader lid brush

dark eye shadow (any color)

black pencil eyeliner

black eye shadow

medium eye shadow (same shade as dark shadow)

highlight eye shadow color

black mascara

Learn the secret to this classic look, and you'll never pay to get your makeup done again. Make it dramatic by going extra dark, or keep it casual with lighter shades.

STEPS:

1. Use your middle finger to apply eye shadow primer to your top lids.

2. Use the medium-sized eye shadow brush to apply the dark eye shadow to your top eyelid. Blend it from the outer edge of your lashes almost to your inner eye, and up to where the crease in your eyelid might be. If you don't have a crease, just blend about halfway up.

3. Apply the black eyeliner to the waterline of your lower lid. Your waterline is the edge inside your lashes.

4. Use the shader lid brush to apply the black eye shadow below your lower lashes, blending very well.

STYLE TIP:
IF YOU DON'T HAVE A SHADER LID BRUSH, DON'T PANIC. JUST USE A COTTON SWAB.

5. Use the small eye shadow brush to apply the black eye shadow to your outer upper eyelid and along the lashes about ²/₃ of the way into the eye. Then continue blending to drag some of the black shadow out and slightly up toward the outer edge of your eyebrow.

6. Use the medium eye shadow brush to apply the medium eye shadow along and slightly above the crease of your eyelid. This will help blend from the deep, dark browns and blacks to the color of your natural skin.

7. Use your medium eye shadow brush to apply the highlight color to the inner corner of your eye. Then use it just under your eyebrow arch.

8. Finish by applying black mascara to both the top and bottom lashes.

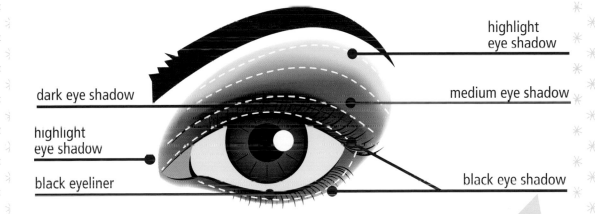

highlight eye shadow

medium eye shadow

dark eye shadow

highlight eye shadow

black eye shadow

black eyeliner

STYLE TIP:
EYE SHADOW PRIMER IS A NEUTRAL PRODUCT YOU CAN APPLY TO YOUR EYELIDS TO HELP YOUR EYE SHADOWS STAY PUT ALL DAY. IF YOU DON'T HAVE PRIMER, JUST DAB ON A LITTLE CONCEALER INSTEAD.

HI THERE, BRIGHT EYES!

The smoky eye was dark and dramatic, but this look is bright and spunky. Experiment with your favorite colors to get the perfect look for you.

STEPS:

1. Use your middle finger to apply eye shadow primer to your top lids.

2. Use a medium-sized eye shadow brush to apply white eye shadow across your whole eyelid.

3. Use the medium-sized brush to apply the yellow eye shadow across your entire lid about ⅔ of the way up.

4. Dust off the brush, and apply a layer of orange shadow on top of the yellow. Make sure to leave a line of yellow showing just under the eyebrow.

5. Dust off the brush again and layer bright pink shadow over the orange from the lash line up to the crease of the eyelid.

6. Use the small eye shadow brush to add a swipe of navy eye shadow to the outer corner of your lower lid.

7. Dust off the brush, and blend blue along the inner edge of the navy.

8. Dust off the brush again, and apply neon green along the inner edge of the blue.

9. Use your finger to add a dab of shimmer powder around the inner edges of your eyes.

10. Apply black eyeliner above your top lashes.

11. Apply black mascara to both your top and bottom lashes.

POWER BROWS

Thick, dramatic brows will draw attention to your captivating eyes. Follow this tutorial to get your brows just right. Highlight what you have and fill in what you don't. Then strike a powerful pose.

WHAT YOU NEED:

tweezers
eyebrow brush or clean toothbrush
eyebrow pencil

STEPS:

FIRST MAP OUT YOUR BROWS

Use this simple trick when you tweeze your brows to be sure they are shaped correctly.

1. Hold your eyebrow pencil vertically with the bottom end touching the outside of your right nostril. The top of the pencil will show you where your inner eyebrow should begin.

2. Keep the bottom of the eyebrow pencil touching your outer nostril. Tilt the top end of the pencil outward. Pause when the pencil is in front of the colored part of your eye. The place where the pencil touches your eyebrow is where your arch should be.

3. Now tilt the pencil again. This time the pencil is just below the outer edge of your lower lashes. The top of the pencil will point to where your brow should end.

NOW FILL THEM IN!

1. Use your eyebrow brush or clean toothbrush to brush your eyebrow hairs up toward your hairline.

2. Draw light lines throughout your eyebrows with the eyebrow pencil to fill them in. These lines should mimic the growth of your own eyebrow hairs.

3. Use your eyebrow brush to blend the pencil lines into your own brows.

CHOOSING THE RIGHT EYEBROW PENCIL COLOR

BRUNETTES: Find a pencil that matches the lightest parts of your hair.

RED HEADS: Try to find a slightly ashy or slightly gray version of your hair color.

BLACK HAIR: Cool, medium browns work best.

BLONDES: Match your eyebrows to the darkest parts of your hair.

LASH OVERLOAD

False lashes can take your makeup game to the next level. With a little practice, you'll be popping them on in no time.

There are different types of false lashes. Full strip lashes are bold and beautiful. Individual or clustered lashes offer a more subtle look. Play around with different types to find the lashes you love the most. Just remember to proceed with caution! Using glue and tweezers near your eyes can be dangerous. Make sure you are very careful.

STEPS:

1. Measure the false lashes to fit your eye. Hold them up along your upper eyelashes. If they are too wide, just snip off the excess from the outer corner.

2. Hold the center of the lashes with your tweezers as you apply the glue along the adhesive edge. If the glue does not come with an easy applicator, just dip a bobby pin into it and use the tip of the bobby pin to carefully apply the glue to the edge of the false lashes. Wait a few seconds for the glue to get tacky.

3. Use the tweezers to very slowly and carefully set the lashes down on top of your eyelashes in the center. Then, carefully slide the lashes all the way back until they bump into your eyelid. Use your fingers to press the outer and inner edges of the lashes into place.

STYLE TIP:
ONCE YOU'RE CONFIDENT WITH YOUR FALSE LASH APPLICATION SKILLS, MIX IT UP! GLUE RHINESTONES OR TINY STUDS ALONG YOUR LASH LINE FOR EXTRA DRAMA.

CAPTIVATING CAT EYES

Cat eyes are an iconic look that scream, "Drama!" They're also a bit tricky. Don't spend hours in front of the mirror frustrated that you aren't getting the dramatic sweep just right. Cat eyes can actually be very quick and easy. Follow these steps for the purrfect look.

WHAT YOU NEED:

masking tape
liquid eyeliner
thin eye shadow brush
makeup remover
mascara

STEPS:

1. Apply a small piece of masking tape running from your outer lower lashes up toward the area just past the outer edge of your brow.

2. Paint the liquid liner along the edge of the piece of tape as high as you'd like. It's a good idea to start with a short line and see how you like it.

3. Use the liquid liner to draw a line from the inner edge of your top lashes all the way to the end of the line you've created with the tape.

4. Fill in the eyeliner to create a thick black line along your lashes.

5. Dip your eye shadow brush in your makeup remover. Use it to clean up any uneven areas along your cat eye.

6. Apply mascara to the top and bottom lashes.

STYLE TIP:
KEEP YOUR MAKEUP REMOVER HANDY WHEN YOU'RE LEARNING TO USE LIQUID EYELINER. IF YOU DON'T HAVE ANY, COLD CREAM WILL DO THE TRICK. JUST SLATHER IT ON AND USE A TISSUE OR COTTON BALL TO WIPE IT OFF.

ROCK THOSE MATTE SHADES

WHAT YOU NEED:

gentle facial cleanser
clean toothbrush
concealer
lip liner
matte black, blue, or deep purple lipstick
tissues
translucent powder
small makeup brush

You can paint them pink, red, purple, or even black. Your lips speak volumes, even if you don't say a word!

Matte lip colors have no shimmer or shine. Getting a vivid matte lip color to stay put isn't easy, especially if its black, blue, or deep purple. These dark hues tend to fade, bleed, or smudge. A few simple tricks will change all that. Get the long-lasting lip look you'll love.

STEPS:

1. Wash your lips with the gentle cleanser. Use your clean toothbrush to gently rub off any dead skin. Dry thoroughly.

2. Apply concealer all over your lips, including the area surrounding them. Blend well.

3. Carefully line your lips along your lip line with the lip liner.

4. Apply your lipstick, making sure to stay within the lip liner.

5. Hold a tissue up to your lips. Dip your makeup brush into the translucent powder, and gently tap it onto the tissue over your lips. Doing this should set your lipstick so that it will stay put for longer.

STYLE TIP:
BECOME A LIP LINER PRO! APPLY THIS PENCIL-LIKE PRODUCT IN LIGHT, SHORT STROKES ALONG THE EDGES OF YOUR LIPS. THIS WILL HELP YOU AVOID A HARSH OR UNEVEN LOOK AS YOUR LIPSTICK WEARS OFF.

GLITTER GLAM

Looking to add some extra oomph to your look? Try glitter lips! This sparkling tutorial works for a prima ballerina, an edgy artist, or anyone in between.

STEPS:

1. Apply your lipstick.

2. Blot your lips on the tissue.

3. Apply a second coat of lipstick.

4. Dip the tip of the cotton swab into the water to moisten it, then roll it in the glitter to pick up as much as you can.

5. Tap the cotton swab against your lips to transfer the glitter. Repeat steps 4 and 5 until you've covered your lips with glitter.

6. Press your lips firmly together to help press the glitter into your lipstick.

7. Tear off a small piece of masking tape from the roll and blot it against your skin to pick up any glitter that fell from your lips onto your chin or cheeks.

STYLE TIP:

BE PREPARED! GLITTER LIPS DON'T HAVE MUCH STAYING POWER, SO YOU'LL NEED TO REAPPLY OFTEN. LUCKILY, IT DOESN'T TAKE LONG TO FRESHEN YOUR LIPS. BRING YOUR LIPSTICK, GLITTER, AND A COTTON SWAB WITH YOU.

OMBRÉ LIP

Ombré lips can be as bold or subtle as you want. Experiment with different color combinations and ombré directions to get the look you love.

WHAT YOU NEED:

concealer
lipstick brush
3 lipsticks in different colors
tissues

STEPS:

1. Apply concealer all over and around your lips.

2. Run your lipstick brush across the top of one tube of lipstick to pick up some color.

3. Use the brush to apply this lipstick color to the top half of your top lip.

4. Clean the brush by rubbing it on a tissue, and then apply the next color to the bottom half of your top lip and the top half of your bottom lip. Use the brush to blend the two colors where they meet.

5. Clean the brush again, and fill in the bottom half of your bottom lip with the last color. Again, blend the two colors where they meet.

6. Blot your lips on the tissue.

STYLE TIP:
RESIST THE URGE TO SQUEEZE YOUR TOP AND BOTTOM LIPS TOGETHER! IT WILL RUIN THE OMBRÉ EFFECT.

ANIMAE-ZING MAKEUP

Makeup can be a great way to express yourself! And what is self-expression if not art? If you're ready to take your makeup game to the major leagues, try some more artistic looks. You may have a future in makeup artistry. For this first look, start with a fully contoured face and then boost the look into anime magic!

WHAT YOU NEED:

large makeup brush
blush
tissue
translucent powder
eyebrow pencil
black eyeliner
white eyeliner
black mascara
false lashes
eyelash glue
light pink lipstick

STEPS:

1. Use the large makeup brush to apply blush to the apples of your cheeks. Blend it well.

2. Wipe the large makeup brush off on a tissue. Then use it to apply translucent powder all over your face.

3. Use your eyebrow pencil to fill in your eyebrows. Elongate your eyebrows just a little by adding length to the outer ends with the pencil.

STYLE TIP:
A COLORFUL WIG IS THE PERFECT FINISHING TOUCH FOR THIS COMIC BOOK LOOK.

CONTINUE →

NOW THAT YOU HAVE THE BASE, ADD IN THE COMIC-WORTHY DETAILS!

4. Get out the black eyeliner. Draw the dramatic cat eye on your upper lid.

5. Apply black mascara.

6. Use your white eyeliner to draw a thick line below your lower lashes extending just a bit past your inner eye. Then fill in your lower water line as well.

7. Use the black eyeliner to draw a thin outline below your white eyeliner. This will make your eyes look bigger.

8. Add false lashes to your top eyelids.

9. Apply light pink lipstick to your lips, and blot on a tissue.

STYLE TIP:
IF ANY OF YOUR BLACK LINES AREN'T QUITE AS SMOOTH AS YOU WANT, DIP A COTTON SWAB IN CONCEALER, AND USE IT TO PERFECT YOUR WORK!

GET THE LICHTENSTEIN LOOK

Make yourself a work of comic book art. Roy Lichtenstein was a 1960s pop artist. He became famous for his paintings that looked like comic book illustrations. This jaw-dropping look is sure to win the top prize at any costume party. It's a fun way to finesse your makeup artistry.

WHAT YOU NEED:

foundation
concealer
blue face paint
small paintbrush
black eyeliner
white eyeliner
stencil for circular dots
deep orange eye shadow
small eye shadow brush
red lipstick
makeup remover
black mascara

STEPS:

1. Apply a thin base of foundation to your face. Add concealer under your eyes or on any blemishes.

2. Use the small paintbrush to paint a tear or two in blue paint below one eye. Outline the tears with black eyeliner. Use white eyeliner to add small highlights at the lower corners of each tear.

CONTINUE

STYLE TIP:
THIS LOOK GOES GREAT
WITH A PROP. CREATE
A CARDBOARD WORD
BUBBLE ON A STICK WITH
A FUN CATCH PHRASE.

3. Hold the circle stencil against your skin. Use your small eye shadow brush to fill inside the stencil with orange eye shadow. Repeat in an even pattern all across your face, except for your blue tear and lips.

4. Now do your eyes. Use the black eyeliner to draw an extreme cat eye on your top eyelid. Add a thick line of white eyeliner below your lower lashes and inside your waterline. Add black eyeliner below the white eyeliner.

5. Now add accent lines. Draw an arch just above your eyelid crease with black eyeliner. Add a line along your jawline and your brow line. Draw a straight line down the ridge of your nose, and outline the nostrils.

6. Fill in your eyebrows with the black eyeliner.

7. Apply red lipstick to your lips. Blot on a piece of tissue, and add another coat. Use white eyeliner to paint reflection lines on your top and bottom lips. Line the outsides of your lips with black eyeliner.

8. Finish this look with a coat of black mascara on your top lashes.

STYLE TIP:
FOR SOME CHARACTER, CONSIDER ADDING A WORRIED ARCH OVER ONE OR BOTH BROWS.

POP ART ZOMBAE

Give a comic book look a gory yet glamorous twist. This look combines contouring, pop art, and the classic smoky eye, but it does it all with a zomBAE twist!

STEPS:

1. Use a makeup sponge to apply green face paint all over your face and neck.

2. Blend the green paint with a little black or gray paint on your paper plate to make a darker shade. Use your makeup sponge to apply this color to contour below your cheekbones, below your jaw, and around your hairline. Build up the color until you have the perfect undead look.

3. Use a small paintbrush to draw arched eyebrows with black face paint. The brows should be drawn on above your natural brows.

CONTINUE

4. Apply the black eye shadow liberally with a medium eye shadow brush all around your eyes in a circle. Blend it into the green face paint.

5. Add mascara to both eyes.

6. Using the other shade of green face paint, draw several jagged shapes on half of your face. Make sure one shape goes around the edge of your mouth.

7. Use the black eyeliner to paint edges around the jagged sections. Shade them in to look like rotting flesh.

8. Use black eyeliner to outline two rows of teeth on one side of your lips.

9. On the other side of your lips, use the eyeliner to outline your lips. Use a small paintbrush to fill in the teeth with white or yellow face paint.

10. Fill in the other half of your lips with bright pink lipstick.

STYLE TIP:
FOR A POP OF COLOR, FILL YOUR EYEBROWS IN WITH THE PINK LIPSTICK AND ADD A BRIGHT-COLORED WIG!

ZIPPER FACE MAKEOVER

This hot look is a little gory and a little goth. It's also completely captivating!

STEPS:

1. Cut the fabric edging away from the zipper. Unzip the zipper until only 1 inch (2.5 centimeters) remains zipped.

2. Use the white eyeliner to lightly draw on your face where you'll place the zipper. Make sure your nose, mouth, one eye, and one eyebrow are inside the zipper.

WHAT YOU NEED:

- 8-inch (20-cm) fabric zipper
- scissors
- white eyeliner
- cotton swabs
- spirit gum
- liquid latex
- old paintbrush
- foundation
- makeup sponge
- brow pencil
- black, brown, and gray eye shadow
- black eyeliner
- black mascara
- small and medium makeup brushes
- black and white face paint
- studs and gemstones

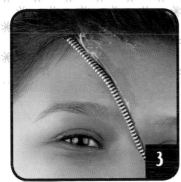

3. For this step, work in sections. Use a cotton swab to apply spirit gum over the white line. Then press the zipper onto the glue. Hold it in place for several seconds to make sure it sticks. Glue the ends of the zipper to the underside of your chin to keep them out of the way.

4. Carefully paint two to three layers of liquid latex along the outer edges of the zipper. Give it plenty of time to dry between coats. This step will help your zipper look like it is blending into your skin.

5. Use the makeup sponge to apply foundation to the areas of your face on the outside of the zipper. Cover the dried latex with foundation.

6. Fill in the eyebrow on the outside of the zipper with the eyebrow pencil. Give yourself a smoky eye on that eye.

CONTINUE

7. Use a small makeup brush to apply white face paint on the inner edges of the zipper. Be careful not to cover the zipper's teeth with paint. Use the medium brush to fill in the inside of the zipper with white paint. Leave a pear-shaped section of skin bare on your nose and a circle around the eye inside the zipper.

8. Rinse and dry the small makeup brush. Then use it to paint a black pear shape over your nose and a black circle over your eye and eyebrow.

9. Carefully use the small brush to draw a black line extending from the corner of your mouth out toward your ear. It should be about 1 inch (2.5 cm) long. Next, draw 10 parallel vertical lines across your lips. These will be your teeth.

10. Wipe the brush off on the paper towel to get rid of most of the black paint. Then use it to round off the tops and bottoms of each tooth. Pull them into points to make the tooth roots. These lines will look a little gray.

11. Clean the small brush and fill inside the teeth with a layer of white paint to make them stand out.

12. Then, use the brush to soften some of the lines above and below your teeth. This will provide some shading to make your teeth look more realistic.

13. Finish your look by using spirit gum to stick gemstones and studs anywhere you want. Try circling your eye or adding a pattern along your cheekbone.

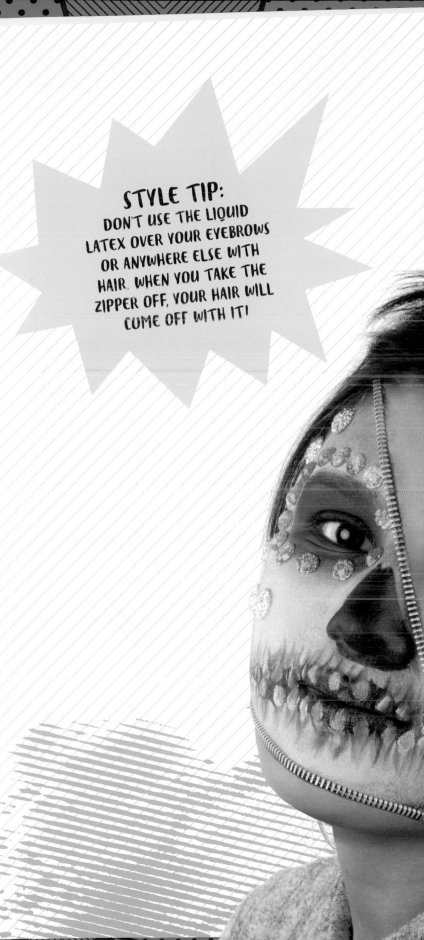

STYLE TIP:
DON'T USE THE LIQUID LATEX OVER YOUR EYEBROWS OR ANYWHERE ELSE WITH HAIR. WHEN YOU TAKE THE ZIPPER OFF, YOUR HAIR WILL COME OFF WITH IT!

MERMAID MAKEUP

You can use makeup to make your fantasies come to life! For an over-the-top look that's sure to make a splash at your next costume party, try this mermaid makeup tutorial. You could even incorporate elements into your everyday makeup routine.

WHAT YOU NEED:

- foundation
- concealer
- eyebrow pencil
- mesh weaving cap or fishnet stockings
- alligator clip
- makeup sponges
- face paint in blue, purple, pink, green, and teal
- eye shadow in purple, blue, yellow, and pink
- small, medium, and large eye shadow brushes
- tissue
- black eyeliner
- mascara
- blue lipstick

STEPS:

1. Apply a thin base of foundation all over your face. Add concealer below your eyes and on any blemishes.

2. Fill in your brows using the eyebrow pencil.

3. Pull the mesh weaving cap or fishnet stockings down snugly over your face. If you need to, secure them with an alligator clip so that the netting is tight.

4. Apply the purple face paint to your hairline and the tops of your cheekbones by tapping the sponge onto your skin over and over.

5. Use the large eye shadow brush to tap on the purple eye shadow on top of the paint to set the color.

6. Use a clean sponge to apply the blue face paint across the top of your forehead and lower down at the top edge of your cheekbones. Clean the eye shadow brush on the tissue, and set that color by tapping matching eyeshadow on top of it.

CONTINUE →

7. Use another clean sponge to add pink face paint below the others on your forehead, blending as you go. Add it along your entire cheekbones. Set it with pink eye shadow.

STYLE TIP:
TO TAKE THIS LOOK UP A NOTCH, TRY ADDING COLORED FALSE EYELASHES THAT MATCH YOUR MERMAID SCALES.

8. Carefully lift the netting away from your face, and pull it off.

9. Use the medium eye shadow brush to apply bright pink eye shadow just above your eyelashes on your top eyelids.

10. Apply the purple eye shadow in an arch through the crease in your eyelid, blending well.

11. Use the small eye shadow brush to apply teal shadow around your tear ducts and below your lower lashes. Blend in yellow and pink for a colorful pop!

12. Apply black eyeliner on the top lid.

13. Add mascara to the top lashes.

14. Apply blue lipstick to your lips. Blot it on a tissue, and add a second layer of blue lipstick.

HALF-GALAXY MAKEOVER

Combine cosmetics with the cosmos for an out-of-this-world look. The dark background makes the white stars pop.

WHAT YOU NEED:

- foundation
- concealer
- flat blush brush
- blue face paint
- eye shadow blending brush
- eye shadow in bright pink, purple, black, and blue
- white shimmer eye shadow pen
- black eyeliner
- black mascara
- purple lipstick

STEPS:

1. Apply a thin base of foundation all over your face. Add concealer below your eyes and on any blemishes.

2. Dip the flat blush brush into the blue face paint. Dab it around the area of your face where you want your galaxy. Add a bit more paint to your brush, and keep dabbing. Gradually build up the blue color, especially in the center of the area.

CONTINUE

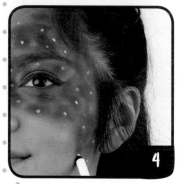

3. Next add colorful swirls to your galaxy. Use the eyeshadow blending brush to apply pink, purple, blue, and black eyeshadow in dotting motions. Blend them out, and add more until you get the swirly look of the cosmos.

4. Add white stars to the clusters by dabbing the white eye shadow pen onto your skin. Add a few larger dabs of white. Then use your finger to gently smudge the dots to one side. They will look like shooting stars.

5. Now make your eyes stand out. Wipe off the eye shadow brush on a tissue. Now, on both eyes, add a bold swipe of purple eye shadow on your top lid. Blend it up into your crease.

6. Wipe off the brush again, and apply bright pink eye shadow onto your non-galaxy eyelid. Blend it up into the crease.

7. Wipe off the brush one last time, and add blue eye shadow next to the pink. Blend it on the inside of the eye around the tear duct.

8. Use the black eyeliner to draw a thick cat eye on your top eyelids.

9. Apply mascara to your top and bottom lashes.

10. Finish your captivating look with bold purple lipstick.

OTHER BOOKS IN THIS SET

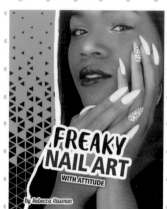

AUTHOR BIO

REBECCA RISSMAN is a nonfiction author and editor. She has written more than 300 books about history, science, and art. Her book *Shapes in Sports* earned a starred review from Booklist, and her series Animal Spikes and Spines received a 2013 Teachers' Choice Award for Children's Books from *Learning Magazine*. Rissman especially enjoys writing about fashion. She studied fashion history as part of her master's degree in English Literature at Loyola University Chicago. She lives in Chicago, Illinois, with her husband and two daughters.